CREEPY
CARMARTHEN

CREEPY CARMARTHEN

NICK BRUNGER

Gomer

First published in 2018 by Gomer Press,
Llandysul, Ceredigion SA44 4JL

ISBN 978 1 78562 210 6

A CIP record for this title is available from the British Library.

© Nick Brunger, 2018

Nick Brunger asserts his moral right under the
Copyright, Designs and Patents Act, 1988
to be identified as author of this work.

This book is published with the financial support of the
Welsh Books Council.

Printed and bound in Wales at
Gomer Press, Llandysul, Ceredigion
www.gomer.co.uk

Acknowledgements

With grateful thanks to those historians past and present who have shared their stories and in particular to the Carmarthenshire Library Service who give everyone access to our wonderful past through the priceless volumes that are to be found on their shelves.

The Carmarthen Journal

Carmarthen Archive Service for their help in sourcing and providing some of the images for this book.

Photograph of Castle House Carmarthen Lock-up © Carmarthenshire Archive Service

Photograph of St Peter's Church tower © Sam Brown

Photographs of the author by kind permission of Carmarthenshire County Council © Aled Llewelyn

Illustration of the Guildhall © Carmarthenshire Archive Service

Introduction

Carmarthen lays claim to being the oldest town in Wales, with a rich and varied history dating back more than two thousand years. You would expect, with such a full past, that we would have a host of wonderful and dramatic stories from those years gone by – and so we do. But the history of Carmarthen also holds some of the weirdest true tales in the country.

The legendary birthplace of Merlin, King Arthur's great wizard, Carmarthen owes its origins to the Romans who created Moridunum – "*the fort by the sea*" – as the base for their legions to subdue the Demetae tribe and guard the lucrative gold mines at Dolaucothi.

Give or take an ancient war or two, the town has been in continuous occupation ever since, with the stones of the invaders' buildings forming the foundations of many of today's properties.

The old town was built around the Roman fort, roughly where Priory Street is today. When the Normans came, they established a new settlement around their castle and, as the population grew, the two settlements merged.

Carmarthen Castle became a place of power and influence, administering both government and justice to southwest Wales.

As a seat of both religious and political power, the town thrived with churches and chapels, an influential priory and the largest Franciscan friary outside London. It was here that the earliest surviving Welsh manuscript, *The Black Book of Carmarthen*, was compiled, recording our country's mythology, history, nature and poetry.

In contrast, this book tells of a more recent past of drunkenness, violence and sinful behaviour; a time when, as its influence declined, the town gained a reputation as being the "Wild West of Wales." Inevitably most of the stories come from the nineteenth century, when local papers began to record in detail in the news of the day and violent behaviour seemed to reach its peak.

Bull-baiting and cock-fighting drew the crowds on streets that were infamous for drunkenness and brawling. Festivals and holidays were marked by rowdiness and mischief with gun-shots, fireworks and burning barrels of tar rolled through the streets.

One hundred and fifty pubs served drink at all hours of the day and well into the night, supplying a thirsty populous swelled by the sailors who plied their trade in the town's busy port. Gambling thrived and prostitutes, sometimes called the "nymphs of the pavement," did a roaring trade.

Election times were often catalysts for rioting and voter intimidation, with the local population lining up to support the Blues and the Reds, political parties who divided the loyalty of the townspeople and gave their names to two of the streets. Woe betide anyone who inflamed the mob, who could retaliate by demolishing your house, beating you senseless or offering to put out your eyes if you showed support for their opponents.

The law struggled to keep control despite a host of cruel sanctions against those it considered criminals. Deportation, flogging, execution and imprisonment were the tools employed, and some two hundred offences carried the death penalty.

Hangings were a popular entertainment, attracting such huge crowds that executions had to take place in the countryside to find room for the thousands who came to watch the punishments carried out.

Highwaymen and murderers paid for their crimes at the ends of the rope, but so did petty thieves, larcenous teenagers and the insane.

Corruption was rife, bribery commonplace and it was accepted that a wealthy man could buy votes from the electorate or swing the verdict of the court.

This book draws on the stories taken from those times, but also looks at other weird and wonderful fragments from the past: soldiers who made their mark on British history, but whose stories have elements that we would all recognise as being decidedly creepy; why our first police force was nicknamed "the Carmarthen Shilling;" and whether

Jack the Ripper's last victim once walked the streets of our town.

There are tales taken from the sea, strange facts about the past and weird links with incidents from British history that take us back as far as medieval times.

I began collecting these stories when I moved to Carmarthenshire, seeking at first to find out more about my new home. Discovering our truly weird and wonderful history, I began telling these tales in my guided walk "The Creepy Carmarthen Tour," and was gratified to find that others shared my interest in these oddities from the past.

Although I designed the walk with the tourist trade in mind, I have been delighted to discover that the stories appeal just as much to local people. I hope you enjoy reading them as much as I enjoy telling these terrific tales.

The gallows in the backyard of the Castle House lock up.

Victims
of the
Gallows

No horrible history of Carmarthen can ignore the part that the hangman has played in our past, nor the fascination our ancestors had with the gallows. Centuries ago, local people turned out in their thousands to see a good hanging. Even after judicial executions moved to within the walls of the prison, hundreds would crowd around the gates waiting for the prison bell to toll and the black flag to be hoisted over the entrance to show that the deed had been done.

No execution attracted more attention than that of Edward Higgins, thought to be among the last of the eighteenth century's notorious highwaymen.

When Higgins went to the gallows on September 7th 1767, he was dressed more like a bridegroom than a man preparing to be hanged. Wearing a brand-new suit of clothes and a flower in his buttonhole, he was watched by a vast crowd standing around Babell

Hill at Pensarn as the executioner placed the noose around his neck.

Higgins' freshly tailored outfit was more than a show of bravado to the mob who always attended such events. The new clothes were also a bribe to the hangman: the executioner had it in his powers to make a man's exit from this world swift or slow. Make the "drop" too short and the condemned man could struggle at the end of the rope for a considerable time as he slowly choked to death. A longer drop aimed to break the victim's neck and bring about a merciful end. In some cases, the hangman who had been bribed would leap onto the back of the prisoner or pull on their legs to hasten their death.

Although paid just a pittance for carrying out the execution, the hangman's "perks" included the right to auction off the dead man's clothes, as well as sell sections of the noose as souvenirs. The highwayman's fine clothes would fetch a good price from a local landlord, who would put the items on display in the bar-room.

Higgins' chequered criminal career had begun in Worcester, where he was sentenced to seven years' transportation to America for housebreaking. No sooner had he arrived in Boston than he escaped custody, robbed a wealthy merchant and adopted a fresh identity in order to buy a passage back to England.

The stolen cash also bought him a fine house in Cheshire where he took a young wife and adopted the style of a country squire, riding to hounds and living a life of idleness and luxury. His wife became accustomed to his many absences on business, not realising that his real trade was now highway robbery with a little high-class burglary on the side.

When the law finally caught up with him, he escaped custody again and fled to Bristol where he posed as a wealthy gentleman. To avoid being recognised in his home town, he travelled throughout the south-west of England and Wales to carry out his many crimes, including the murder of an elderly woman and her maid.

His downfall came at Laugharne, where he was caught in the act of burglary at the home of Lady Maud and Madam Bevan. He managed to wrestle with the locals who tried to apprehend him, but one had a dog that bit him and held on until he was taken into custody.

His wife Katherine did all she could to save her man. Before and during the trial, she was seen frequently walking the streets of Carmarthen dressed in white as a sign of her husband's innocence, hoping to influence the judge and jury. Once he had been sentenced to death, she made one last desperate attempt to free him from gaol. She forged a letter from the Home Secretary granting a reprieve from the gallows and had an accomplice travel to Brecon to put it onto the Carmarthen-bound mail coach. However, an official at the prison spotted that the London postmark was missing and recognised the letter to be a forgery.

On the day of his execution, Higgins was due to walk from the gaol in Carmarthen Castle across the bridge over the Towy to the gallows. Instead he chose to run along the route, with the prison governor, priest and escort all desperately trying to keep up with him, much to the amusement of the crowd.

Although he had strenuously denied any wrongdoing at his trial and made a speech on the gallows claiming to be innocent of the charges against him, as he was stripped of his clothes after the hanging, officials found a letter in his pocket confessing not only to highway robbery but also to several counts of murder.

And there is one more gory twist to the tale.

In bygone days, the death sentence ordered that the condemned man or woman should be "hung, drawn and quartered." This referred to the horribly cruel process of hanging the prisoner until they were insensible, then cutting them down and reviving them. The executioner, often a local butcher, would then "draw" out their innards, cutting open the stomach and pulling out their guts while the prisoner was still alive. The body was then cut into quarters and the body parts, including the head, put on display around the county.

By the time Higgins died, this horrible practice had ended, but after execution the victims of the gallows were usually "anatomised" – that is, their corpse was dissected in front of a paying public. However, in Higgins' case a deal had been done to sell his body on to a London surgeon called Cruikshank who wanted to use the body for his apprentices (as medical students were then called) to dissect.

To ensure the corpse was as little damaged as possible, the surgeon had paid for the body to be cut down from the gallows quickly rather than leaving it on display for an hour or so for the crowd to inspect, as was usually the case. On opening up the body, it was discovered that Higgin's heart was still beating! Although he had been declared dead on the gallows by the doctor, he had survived the execution. It was left to one of the surgeon's assistants to quietly complete the sentence of the court.

While the huge crowd who had attended Higgins' execution was unaware of the botched hanging, the thousands who stood on Spilman Street to watch David Evans die on Monday 21st September 1829 unfortunately bore witness to a similarly macabre spectacle. Mercifully, this was to be the last public execution carried out in Carmarthen.

Evans had been courting Hannah Davies for some time and most people who knew them believed that they might marry. One Saturday evening in June, Hannah set out to walk over the mountain from her employer's home at Rhiwsaithbren to her father's house at Tanygar.

The next morning a walker came across her body lying beside a stream. Thinking that she was asleep, he went to wake her, only to discover to his horror that she was lying in a pool of blood. She had been stabbed and struck around the head with a cleaver and her body dragged to the water's edge in an attempt to conceal it.

The police search for her killer soon found the culprit; Evans had been seen running from the scene in an agitated fashion and his shoes matched footprints found at the murder scene.

At his trial he denied any part in Hannah's murder, but after conviction admitted that he had killed her with his billhook, which he had carried concealed under his coat for just such a purpose.

Why Evans killed Hannah was never established, but the girl was found to be two months' pregnant at the time of her death. The murderer denied any knowledge of this fact, but her sister interrupted his trial to call out: "You villain! She did tell you so and you asked her to wait a month longer to know if she was really pregnant."

Up until the end of the eighteenth century, executions in Carmarthen took place at either Pensarn or on the common at Johnstown. However, since the building of the new prison in the castle grounds, the gallows had found a new home over the gateway facing Spilman Street, some thirty feet up in the air.

Modern executions had done away with the ladder or stool from which the prisoner was "turned off," and now he stood over a trapdoor with the noose attached to a crossbeam overhead.

At a signal from the prison governor, the trapdoor opened, and Evans fell – not to his death, but to the prison roof beneath his feet. Contemporary details are sketchy, but it is thought that either the noose had not been tied properly in place or that the beam holding the noose had collapsed.

There was a common belief at the time that a failed execution was a sign from God that the convicted man was innocent; the Carmarthen crowd believed this and called out for the execution to be halted.

Hoping that his life would be spared, Evans screamed in broken English: "No hang again. No. No. No. No gentleman was ever hung twice." However, the hangman is reported to have said in reply: "No, sir, you are mistaken. I have sworn my duty to hang you by the neck until you are dead. So up you go and down you drop, and may the Lord have mercy on your soul."

Once the gallows had been repaired, the hanging was carried out again, this time to the executioner's complete satisfaction.

By the 1820s executions had become much less common. Serious offenders were far more likely to be sentenced to transportation to Australia than to face the gallows. However, things were very different in the previous century when as many as two hundred separate offences could mean a trip to the gallows.

For example, just one month in 1739 saw a man named Edwards hanged for pilfering, while a May Williams was strung up for the murder of her child. On the same day as her execution, two teenagers were hanged for stealing cider from the Greyhound Inn in Carmarthen.

Not every executioner was a trained professional, and on occasion the authorities enlisted fellow prisoners when no-one else could be found to do the job.

One nineteen-year-old convict was granted his freedom in return for carrying out a triple execution in Carmarthen. It must have been a terrifying experience for the young man, who had been given no training in the art of the executioner.

Shortly after his release, the young man was put on trial for another offence and was himself sentenced to death. Now fully aware of the horrors of that lay in store for him, he chose to end his own life instead, cheating the gallows by committing suicide in his cell.

On another occasion, a prison inmate who had been sentenced to fourteen years' transportation to America offered to act as hangman on the condition that his punishment be halved. He was granted his wish and the execution took place at Pensarn without a hitch.

The gallows was a prefabricated affair, stored in the gaol between hangings. After sentence had been carried out, the body was usually left dangling from the noose for an hour or more to ensure that death had occurred, and to allow the crowds to inspect it. The corpse was then cut down and taken away on the prison cart for public dismemberment. The wagon would then return to dismantle the gallows and take it back for storage. However, on one such return journey, it was discovered that the gallows had vanished – stolen by locals who used the wood to make items of furniture.

If hanging seems horribly cruel to our modern minds, spare a thought for women prisoners, who were often burnt at the stake for committing murder. That was the fate of the wife of Wil Goch, who was burnt to death in Carmarthen's Market Place in 1665 for killing her husband.

At least after death her body would have been destroyed. Others of those executed faced yet another indignity. Their corpses were put on display in metal cages called "gibbets" close to the scene of their crimes. Among them was Wil Mani, who was the cause of a one-man crime-wave on Pembrey Mountain during the latter half of the eighteenth century.

His criminal career began while he was still a boy, encompassing highway robbery, sheep and cattle rustling, and wrecking ships. Wil was one of the infamous "hatchet men" who lured ships onto the treacherous and deadly sand bank at Cefn Sidan in Carmarthen Bay, murdering survivors and stealing the cargoes of the unfortunate vessels. Hatchet men took their name from the small axes they used to both smash open the sea chests and barrels that were their booty and to finish off their unfortunate victims.

Mani had married a local farmer's daughter, a pretty girl called Mari who disapproved of his life of crime. He did his very best to go straight, but his efforts ended in failure, and when he returned to his evil ways, Mari left him. Now homeless, she took refuge with a local woman called Margaret Davies who had always been kind to her.

One night, Mani took his cruel revenge on the old woman. Knowing that she was in her home alone, he confronted her, demanding that she should return his wife to their former home. When Mrs Davies refused, he savagely beat out her brains with a milking stool. Unknowingly, he left behind a vital piece of evidence: in her frantic struggle to escape his clutches, Margaret had torn off part of the cuff of his coat.

Eight Carmarthen men were sworn in as special constables to arrest Margaret's killer and they searched high and low, only to find Wil Mani supping ale in a local pub, his dog lying at his feet. He denied all knowledge of the crime, but one of the constables noticed that his coat was missing a portion of the cuff. The villain was arrested and taken off to face justice in Carmarthen.

He paid for his crime on the gallows at Pensarn, struggling and cursing with the hangman as he died, and then, as was often the case, his body was taken down to be "gibbeted" at a crossroads close to the scene of the murder.

First the body was encased in tar to preserve it, then it was welded into an iron cage. This was displayed from a set of gallows as an example to others contemplating a life of crime.

Over time the corpse slowly rotted away, the flesh eaten away by maggots, who in turn became a swarm of flies around the body. To this day, locals talk of a plague of flying insects as being "Wil Mani's flies."

One man who had been a victim of Mani's in the past took special interest in the gibbet. He kept watch over the weeks as the bones began to fall away from the corpse onto the ground. First the fingers and toes, then the larger bones, until finally one of the thighbones came loose from the remaining skeleton.

According to legend, he took that bone and whittled it with a knife, turning it into a pipe which he kept behind the bar in one of Carmarthen's many ale houses, taking great delight in smoking "Wil Mani's Pipe" while supping a pint.

Murder
Most Foul

By the early years of the nineteenth century, attitudes to crime and to criminals had begun to change. Up to that point, Britain's so-called "Bloody Code" had meant that some two hundred and twenty crimes were punishable by death.

Many of those offences had been introduced during the early part of the previous century when the Black Act of 1723 added fifty new capital crimes such as petty theft and poaching to protect the property of the emerging middle classes in Britain.

"There is no country on the face of the earth in which there have been so many different offences according to law to be punished with death," declared MP Sir Samuel Romilly during a debate on the subject in the House of Commons in 1810.

In practice it meant that people could go to the gallows for stealing property worth as little as a shilling. Carmarthen juries, like others across the country, became reluctant to convict offenders for such petty crimes. Often quite major offenders were acquitted, against the evidence presented in court, rather than found guilty and faced with a death sentence.

Judges were also commuting sentences, when the law allowed this, and ordering convicts to be transported to penal colonies such as Australia as an alternative to hanging. In April 1804, Martha Davies found herself in front of the Carmarthen Sessions held in the Guildhall and was punished by transportation for seven years for the theft of three blankets.

However, during the same court hearings, sixty-six-year-old John Morris was sentenced to death for stealing a horse, the property of Evan Price. His sentence was "respited" – postponed – for two months while the judge considered commuting the punishment to either transportation or life imprisonment. Despite numerous petitions from the public, he was hanged at Old Oak Common on June 16th.

By the middle of the nineteenth century there were just five offences that still carried the death penalty for civilians: murder, treason, espionage, arson in the royal dockyards and piracy. Those executions that still took place were now carried out behind the prison walls instead of in public. Here in Carmarthen just three men went to the gallows, and all for murder, before the prison closed in 1922. The first of those executions, using the "scientific drop" designed to kill instantly, took place on 13th March 1888.

The previous November, Thomas Davies was walking on his way from the bank in the centre of Llanelli to the Dafen Tinworks. Across his shoulders he carried a leather satchel containing some £590 in gold and silver coins to pay that week's wages.

On a field footpath at Bryngwyn Hill, David Rees and an unnamed accomplice attacked Mr Davies with a hanger, a tool used in the tinworks, stole £300 from the bag and left him dying on the footpath. A young boy, W.J. Lewis, was playing nearby and hid in a hedge to observe the killing; later, he was able to identify Rees to the police as one of the murderers.

It took the jury at the Guildhall just thirty minutes to reach their verdict of guilty. When asked if he had anything to say before sentence was passed, Rees remained silent. He had always denied carrying out the murder and told the police that he had acted alone, refusing to admit the existence of his accomplice. Placing the customary black cap over his wig, the judge pronounced the death sentence and ordered that Rees should be taken down.

However, once back in the cells. Rees began to shout, complaining loudly that he had not understood the sentence of the court nor the fact that he had been sentenced to hang.

As was customary, the court proceedings had been held in English with a Welsh-language interpreter, Mr Long Price, to translate if it were needed during the trial. Perhaps believing that the outcome was glaringly obvious, he had neglected to explain to Rees that he was to die.

The hundreds waiting outside the courtroom in Guildhall Square would have been in no doubt about the outcome. The bells of the old, long demolished St Mary's Church, which hung behind the Guildhall just under the roofline, would have rung to let people know that the verdict was about to be announced and they would have flocked to the scene. Those watching from the windows overlooking the courthouse would have been able to see the judge place the black cap on his head and passed the word to those gathered below. Cheers from the crowd acknowledged the outcome of the trial.

Rees was brought back into the courtroom and the Judge repeated the sentence as Mr Price whispered his words into the condemned man's ears. Many of the court, including the interpreter, broke down in tears as Rees was led away.

Awaiting execution, Rees declared himself to be "Picil trist" – a sad state of affairs – but did sign a confession that he had acted alone in killing the wages clerk. At the same time, he continued telling his visitors in Carmarthen Prison that he was innocent of the murder. Perhaps the unnamed accomplice had been the man who struck the fatal blow?

David Rees was executed by James Berry, who was, like many of his calling, an eccentric character. He often wore unusual headgear when carrying out his duties, and at Carmarthen Gaol he chose to sport a Turkish fez of the kind later made famous by the comedian Tommy Cooper.

The weeping murderer had to be virtually carried to the gallows by two prison warders. They also supported him on the trapdoor as Berry adjusted the rope around his neck. The apparatus had been used once before at Dolgellau, while the noose, described by the executioner as the best he had ever seen, had been used on four previous occasions.

The prison bell had begun to toll in the ten minutes preceding the execution and, once the deed had been done, a black flag was flown from the flagstaff over the prison gateway as a signal to the waiting crowd. Finally, a notice of execution was posted outside. After death had been certified, Rees' body was buried in quicklime to speed up decomposition. His unmarked grave was in the prison garden, against the wall of the gaol constructed by the architect John Nash. His body remains there today, under the car park of the present-day County Hall.

Carmarthen's final two executions both took place in the same year, 1894. The first to die was George Thomas, a twenty-five-year-old former soldier, for the murder of fifteen-year-old Mary Jane Jones.

Thomas had been seen running along Lammas Street on the evening of November 19th 1893, before approaching a patrolling police constable. He appeared to be plucking up courage to speak, but lost his nerve and continued to run, meeting Sergeant James Jones on King Street a few minutes later. Now he confronted the policeman and told him that he had just committed a murder. At first the sergeant thought it was a joke but, when Thomas persisted, took him for questioning to the police station on Cambrian Place.

By the light of the gas lamps it was clear that Thomas' hands and clothes were covered in blood. The police then searched the area close to the Joint Counties Lunatic Asylum (the grim building on St David's Park that still survives, housing NHS staff at Johnstown) where the murderer told them Mary Jane's body could be found. She was discovered lying in the pool of blood on the country lane midway between Pentremeurig Farm and her home at Dawelan cottage where she lived with her aunt, Mrs Rosie Dyer. She had deep gashes to her throat and her head was virtually cut from her body. The murder weapon, a long, black-handled razor, was found nearby.

The police surgeon, Dr Thomas, reported: "There must have been a terrible struggle, for the tips of the fingers were cut all to pieces by her attempting to clutch the razor with which the crime was committed, and her right thumb was almost severed. It was the most awful sight I have ever seen."

Investigations revealed that Thomas had formed an unhealthy infatuation with Mary Jane, who was a very pretty girl, intelligent and popular with a wide circle of friends. Thomas had made his feelings known to the girl, but she had continually spurned his affections, telling her friends that she was frightened of him.

On the afternoon of the killing, he had been lying in wait for her near the asylum. He forced himself on her, demanding, "give me a sweet kiss," which, as she told her friend Mary Morris, she had refused. The girls spent some time together in Johnstown before Mary Jane set off for home, accompanied for some of the way by her younger brother. It was the last time that she was seen alive.

When he was brought before the magistrates the following day, the police had to force a pathway through a hostile crowd, baying for Thomas' blood and shouting "lynch him, murder him!" But the murderer appeared indifferent to the court proceedings, remarking, "I do not care for this sort of thing."

Thomas came from a respectable local family, and they now disowned their son. He wrote many letters to them from the condemned cell in Carmarthen Prison begging for some contact or a visit from his father, but John Thomas refused to see him. Eventually his step-mother agreed to visit and was asked if she could provide him with spare clothes and newspapers to read, but she refused, telling him that the Bible was of more use in his hour of need.

At his trial, the jury was asked to consider whether Thomas was sane at the time he carried out the killing. The prison governor gave evidence that "he was perfectly calm and to all appearances rational. He is the most callous prisoner I have ever known." The jury agreed, declaring him "guilty and sane."

As the judge passed the death sentence, Thomas remained composed and unruffled as he had done throughout the trial, without showing the slightest sign of compassion or remorse at the killing.

The Guildhall – scene of many murder trials.

Thomas' father John worked at the iron foundry in Carmarthen and was said to have forged the bolt that held the trapdoor in place on the new set of gallows at the gaol, thereby playing an unwitting part in his son's execution. That apparatus was used for the final time in November 1888 when Billington made a return visit to Carmarthen to carry out the execution of Thomas Richards.

A sailor by trade, Richards was due to leave Swansea Harbour on a voyage, but shortly before the ship was due to sail he asked his captain for leave, claiming an urgent appointment at the hospital. Instead he made his way to the home of his sister-in-law Mary Davies in Borth. Mary's husband James was a fellow sailor and Richards knew that the woman would be alone in her home. He travelled to Aberystwyth by train and then stole a pony from a field close to the railway station and rode it bareback all the way to Borth.

He broke into the house at night and, in ransacking the place, woke Mary. To stifle her screams he put a pillow across her face, suffocating her. He later told the court that he was overcome by remorse at this point, but nevertheless was still callous enough to steal her wedding ring, which she had worn on her finger at all times, refusing even to remove it when washing.

An incompetent thief, he was caught using the poor woman's bankbook to try to steal her savings of around £260. When the police searched him, they found Mary's gold ring in his pocket.

He tried to wriggle out of responsibility for the crime, claiming he was at sea at the time of the murder and that he had bought the ring for thirty shillings. However, while awaiting execution in Carmarthen Prison, he made a full confession, claiming that he was drunk throughout the whole of his journey to commit the murder, including his long trek on horseback in the dark.

Richards' wife and son visited him in gaol a few days before his death. The whole family had wept bitterly together, a scene the warders described as touching. The heart-rending sound of his son's keening could be heard throughout the prison as they parted, to the distress of everyone, both staff and prisoners.

James Billington's arrival in Carmarthen to carry out the execution brought crowds onto the streets keen to see what the man looked like. The interest was even greater by the time he left to catch the train back to Manchester, and he was reported to be frightened by their boisterous attention.

A hairdresser by trade, hanging was Billington's part-time job. He was plagued by reporters who were fascinated by his macabre calling and were often among the mob who followed him after a hanging; he took his revenge when they called in for a shave at his shop and bombarded him with questions, bringing his razor to halt half-way across their throat and letting it linger there before leaving half the face unshaven.

Oddly enough, Carmarthen can lay claim to having an official national hangman of its own. Despite its macabre nature, there were always applicants for the post who had to pass a stringent application process to be considered. Before being given full responsibility, they were expected to spend time acting as the executioner's assistant.

One such individual was Robert Ricketts Evans, the son of a Carmarthen solicitor. "Evans the Hangman" became fascinated by the gallows from an early age and managed to talk the notorious executioner William Calcraft into taking him on as an apprentice.

Calcraft was the longest serving member of that sinister brotherhood, carrying out more than three hundred executions during his long career, which began with flogging convicts at Newgate Prison in London. Evans developed a refinement to the hanging process that he claimed was more humane.

"I have attended nearly all the principal ones that have taken place in this kingdom," he wrote to the Home Secretary in 1875, "giving my advice and assistance to the executioner. In no single instance where I have been present has the slightest failure occurred or any unnecessary suffering been caused to the unfortunate culprit. In cases where I have acted alone - in triple executions as at Liverpool and Gloucester - my plans have been completely successful."

However, just like his mentor Calcraft, it seems that he was not quite as skilled as he claimed, and one of the victims of his triple execution was slowly strangled because Evans miscalculated the drop which was designed to break her neck. Such incompetence could not be tolerated, and Evans' brief career as hangman came to an end.

Although most of Carmarthen's killers ended their lives on the gallows, there was one murderer who was mercifully spared the rope - an eight-year-old girl who, in 1742, faced the charge of killing her brother and sister, aged just six and four.

This country was at war with Spain at the time and local people were warned of the prospect of an invasion from the sea, with a special watch kept along the coast.

The children had heard rumours about the Spaniards and how cruel they were said to be to the people they captured. Adults were killed or enslaved, they said, while children would be eaten alive. One night when the children's parents were away from home, there was a terrific thunderstorm. The youngsters mistook the sound of the thunder for Spanish guns.

Terrified that they might fall victim to the invaders, the little girl decided to take matters into her own hands. Rather than be taken by the Spaniards and suffer the terrible fate that had been forecast, the little girl decided to kill her siblings and then herself.

Using her father's billhook, she was successful in despatching her brother and sister. She then tried to commit suicide by throwing herself into the river, but was saved from drowning by her neighbours.

She was put on trial for the murders in the old courthouse which once stood in the centre of Carmarthen but, because of the sad and unusual circumstances, was discharged by the judge and set free.

WARFARE
&
WARRIORS

Wherever you go in Carmarthen, there is no escaping the town's military past. Guildhall Square is dominated by a striking memorial to the local men who perished fighting the Boer War. Lammas Street has a monument marking the sacrifice of the Royal Welsh Fusiliers during the war in Crimea, while the old Infirmary on Priory Street has the memorial to our more recent wars. But one of the most colourful of Carmarthen's fighting men has his grave in St Peter's Church.

Sir Rhys ap Thomas was a noted medieval warrior and nobleman who made his mark as the man who killed King Richard III on the battlefield at Bosworth.

Born in Llandeilo, his family supported the Lancastrians during the War of the Roses. Their fortunes suffered after Rhys's father defended Carreg Cennen Castle against the Yorkists, who demolished it in 1461 to prevent its use in the future. A teenaged Rhys fled to exile in France where he became friends with Henry Tudor, the future Henry VII. Young Henry looked up to the older boy, nicknaming him "father."

When Rhys's uncle died and left the young man his lands and fortune, Rhys returned to Carmarthenshire. Now a wealthy landowner, he was approached by other nobles who asked him to join them in open rebellion against the new king, Richard III. Rhys had no love for Richard, but thought the rebels were unlikely to succeed. He refused to join them and made sure that his choice to be loyal to the throne became known. The rebel army was defeated and the king increased his grip on power.

For his loyalty, Richard rewarded Rhys with more land and great wealth – good fortune that he used wisely, subtly increasing his powers. Unlike some other local barons, he lived modestly, and his people liked that. He surrounded himself with poets and musicians and gave generously to those less fortunate. He thrilled the ordinary people with great public events, especially horse races that were attended by thousands.

A skilled rider himself, he often took part in the contests and usually won.

Although without any official position of authority, he enjoyed tremendous power, particularly in Wales. The bards sang of his enormous popularity: "All the Kingdom is the King's," they claimed, "save where Rhys does spread his wings."

Despite Rhys's refusal to take part in the rebellion against him, the king was wary and asked for Rhys's youngest son to be sent to the court as a hostage. But Rhys had no intention of doing as Richard asked. He knew of other warriors whose sons had been murdered by the king if they incurred the monarch's displeasure. Instead, he wrote a long letter pledging loyalty to Richard and making the excuse that, at just four years of age, his son was far too young to leave his mother.

"Besides," Rhys said. "I swear this solemn oath to you. If anyone tries to invade your country, then they'll do it over my belly" - meaning that Rhys would be lying dead upon the ground before he let the King's enemies in.

Meanwhile his old friend Henry Tudor decided that the time was right to mount his own challenge to the throne. He landed in Mill Bay in Pembrokeshire with a small army of mercenaries and called on Rhys to join him. His support was vital to Henry's cause: if Rhys refused to back him, then other warlords in Wales would follow his example. Legend tells us that Rhys refused at first, repeating the sacred oath that he had sworn to Richard.

"Were those your very words?" asked Henry. "You said 'over your belly', but not over your dead body? Then I can help you discharge your oath and still support me." He asked Rhys to stand under Mullock Bridge at Dale while the invader paraded his small army over the top. "There," he said, "now they have marched over your belly!"

Now fully committed to war, Rhys took his own army of sixteen hundred Carmarthenshire men and led them through south Wales, collecting more recruits along the way.

Henry's army, outnumbered three-to-one, clashed with the King's at Bosworth Field in Leicestershire just two weeks after the invasion. At first the battle was a great and bloody scrap between the two opposing armies. Henry Tudor chose to stay towards the rear, leaving the fighting to his more experienced warriors. Frustrated by his army's lack of progress, King Richard saw an opportunity to make a swift end to the conflict. He noticed that Henry was isolated from the main body of his troops, protected by just a small group of bodyguards that included Rhys ap Thomas.

Richard and his own elite group of knights charged towards Henry, seeking to kill their enemy. In the fierce fighting that followed, Richard lost his horse and found himself surrounded by his enemies. Legend tells us that it was Rhys, armed with a battle axe, who struck the fatal blow. The axe smashed into Richard's skull, cutting through to his brains and killing the king.

The story remained little more than a fable until, in 2013, archaeologists discovered Richard's body buried under a car park in Leicester. Examination of the skeleton revealed the legendary fatal axe wound to the skull.

For his part in supporting the new king, Rhys ap Thomas gained even more power and prestige. He

St Peter's Church – site of Rhys ap Thomas's tomb.

went on to become a loyal servant of Henry Tudor's son, King Henry VIII, and was regarded by many as the virtual ruler of south Wales. On his death at the age of seventy-eight, Rhys was buried in the Priory in Carmarthen. When that great building was demolished on the orders of Henry VIII, his tomb was transferred to St Peter's church where it remains today.

In contrast, the grave of a local man who became a great hero of the Napoleonic Wars is to be found not in Carmarthen, but in St Paul's Cathedral. He is the only Welshman to be buried there.

Lieutenant General Sir Thomas Picton was a Pembrokeshire man who made his home in Carmarthenshire and would have chosen to die there if fate had not conspired to call him back to war.

Born in Haverfordwest in 1758, he became an ensign in his father's infantry regiment at the age of just thirteen. Despite his privileged background, Picton proved to be a tough hard-bitten soldier and a firm disciplinarian with a reputation for swearing. Wellington, the great general and politician, declared him to be a "rough foul-mouthed devil as ever lived."

At twenty-five, Captain Picton put down a mutiny among his own soldiers by fighting his way through a mob of rioters and beating the ring-leader senseless.

Like many officers of the time, he was released on half-pay when the army did not require his services and he established a country home, Iscoed, near Ferryside, living the life of a country gentleman there.

Mid-career, he found himself fighting the Spanish in the West Indies and eventually becoming military governor of Trinidad. The island needed a firm hand to deal with mutiny among the slaves and attacks by pirates. Using his customary rough tactics, he dealt severely with both parties and the island enjoyed a period of peace and prosperity. However, his service there ended in scandal.

He was responsible for ordering the arrest and torture of Louisa Calderon, a fourteen-year-old girl of mixed race who was the mistress of a local criminal. He believed that she had evidence that would lead to the man's conviction.

Images of Louisa being picketed – that is, made to stand with one foot on a wooden peg while being hanged by a rope tied around one wrist – were published in all the major British newspapers. Many of those pictures were of a highly salacious nature, showing her dressed in very skimpy clothes. Put on trial for Louisa's torture, Picton was found guilty, but friends funded an appeal and the verdict was reversed. The court found that, although Louisa had indeed been tortured, Spanish law and not British was still in force on Trinidad at the time of the offence, and their legal code allowed suspects to be ill-treated in this way.

Despite the acquittal, Picton's name was mud in polite society, but by the time the trial ended he was once again serving with the army. He joined General Wellington and fought with distinction in the war against Napoleon in the Spanish Peninsula. He was feted as the hero of the battle of Badajoz. Despite being seriously wounded, he and his troops captured the great fortress against overwhelming odds. For his part in the British victory he became a national hero, and the incident of torture was quickly forgotten.

On his return to Carmarthen, he was met by a huge crowd of cheering townspeople who removed the horses from the shafts of his carriage and pulled it themselves through the streets to Queen Street, where he made a speech of thanks and paid for a plentiful supply of ale for all.

With Napoleon defeated, the sixty-two-year old General Picton retired to Iscoed to recover from his wounds and to enjoy life as a civilian, hunting and shooting and fishing. Shortly before he was called to arms for the final time, he was walking with friends through the churchyard in Ferryside when he spotted a freshly dug grave. To their consternation, he threw himself into the hole and declared "this will do for me." They believed he had had a premonition that he did not have long to live.

Napoleon's escape from exile led to Picton's return to the army. The night before he left Carmarthen, the mayor gave a banquet in his honour at Furnace House, now the county library. In his speech the general declared that he was leaving for "A coronet or Westminster Abbey" - in other words, he was facing "death or glory."

According to legend, when he rode to battle at Waterloo three weeks later, his baggage had gone missing. Instead of his fine military uniform, he wore borrowed civilian clothes, with his nightshirt tucked into his trousers, and a battered top hat. In his hand, instead of a sword, he carried a furled umbrella.

In an early stage of the battle he was seriously wounded, but got his batman to bind his wounds so that his men did not realise how badly he was hurt.

With the French about to break through the allied lines, he ordered his three thousand troops to fire a volley from their muskets, then advance with fixed bayonets. He last words were, "Charge, charge! Hurrah, hurrah!" At that moment he was shot through the head, falling to the ground from his horse, whereupon his own soldiers picked his pockets and stole not only his purse but also the spectacles he was wearing.

General Picton was the most senior British officer to die at the Battle of Waterloo. He was buried in the family vault in Hanover Square in London. However, on the death of Wellington some thirty-five years later, someone had the bright idea of reburying Picton next to the great general in his own tomb in St Paul's Cathedral, in the belief that Wellington would have a fellow soldier to go with him as a companion into the afterlife. It was a strange decision to make; although Wellington admired Thomas Picton as a fine soldier, he personally could not stand the man, finding him rough and ill-mannered, preferring the company of more refined officers.

His death was marked by the erection of a fine monument on the street named after him, Picton Terrace. However, the huge construction swiftly crumbled away, unable to withstand the Carmarthen weather. Locals stole parts of the magnificent carved frieze around it, depicting the general's famous battles. One section, which had been built into a garden wall, was rescued in modern times and is now on display in the county museum. The memorial's replacement still stands, although that also had to be rebuilt in the last century for safety reasons.

Carmarthen Corporation commissioned a portrait of General Picton which hangs over the judges' bench in the courtroom at the Guildhall facing, at the other end of the chamber, that of another notable General.

William Nott came from altogether more humble stock than the aristocratic Thomas Picton. His father, landlord of the Ivy Bush Hotel, put up a sign outside his establishment declaring that customers could "eat, drink and pay Nott" to advertise his services.

Early training with the Carmarthen Volunteers gave young William a taste for military life and he took a commission at the age of just eighteen with the army of the Honourable East India Company. Far more professional than the official British Army, Nott was able to gain promotion by virtue of his skills as a commander in the field and as a highly competent administrator.

One of the so-called 'Sepoy Generals', he had a

deep understanding of the Indian people and their rulers which helped to gain "John Company" a reputation for fairness and competence which far outstripped that of the regular army.

Nott blamed the regular army's generals for enraging the local people and their rulers, which led to the massacre of sixteen thousand troops, their families and camp followers during an ill-fated retreat from the Afghan capital of Kabul.

He was sent to wreak revenge on the Afghans, and, achieving a series of brilliant victories, became a national hero and received a knighthood as a reward.

By the age of sixty-three, he had planned his retirement with great care, and proposed to stay with his brother at his home on Picton Terrace while his own house was being built in Johnstown.

He arrived in Carmarthen to a hero's welcome, and found the streets festooned with ribbons and flowers and the church bells ringing in his honour. However, the welcoming crowds were shocked at the General's appearance. "Sir William … looked fatigued and ill and was scarcely able to bear the excitement of the scene," reported the *Carmarthen Journal*.

An official address by the mayor reduced the poor man to tears and he was only able to whisper a reply. Too ill to attend the dinner arranged in his honour, he tried to speak to the crowds from his brother's doorstep, but was again overcome by emotion. He never left the house. Three months later he died, victim of the wounds he had received during his long career and the many illnesses he had suffered during his service overseas.

His statue, cast in bronze from a cannon captured at the battle of Maharajpur, now stands in the old Market Square that was renamed in his honour in 1845.

CASTLES,
CAVALIERS,
&
CONVICTS

O ne of the first sights that visitors see as they approach Carmarthen is the imposing silhouette of County Hall. The huge stone-faced building, modeled in the style of a French chateau, squats over the remaining walls and towers of Carmarthen Castle. A grand example of Civic Architecture to some – a blot on the landscape to others – County Hall serves as a constant reminder of the town's position as a hub of political power and influence for more than two thousand years.

The first settlement in Carmarthen was established during the Roman invasion of Britain. It is thought that a temporary army camp was constructed during the early days of Roman rule, occupying a rectangular site that stretched from the corner of King and Queen Streets down towards The Parade. As the invaders' hold on the land increased, they created Moridunum – "*the fort by the sea*" – as a base for its legions to subdue the native Demetae tribe. It also helped to guard the lucrative gold mines at Dolaucothi, operated by skilled engineers supported by an army of slaves.

The new fort lay on land between where St Peter's Church now stands and on either side of Priory Street. with the civilian town spreading along the roads beyond the entrance gateways. It was the most westerly town of significance in the Roman Empire (a contemporary travel guide, the *Antonine Itinerary*, described it as "the end of the road") and must have supported a sizable population for the time. Moridunum was large enough to boast an amphitheatre, one of only seven in Britain, capable of holding around five thousand spectators for plays and concerts, sporting events and, of course, occasional displays of gladiatorial combat.

Little is known about Carmarthen's history in the period after the Romans left, but it seems likely that the settlement survived in some form with the buildings cannibalised, ensuring that the "old town" survived up until the Norman conquest and beyond, not being incorporated into larger "new town" until 1546, when it boasted some one hundred houses. Linking them was King Street, a road that can lay claim to being one of the oldest continually occupied street in Wales. Despite its modern Welsh name of Heol y Brenin (the King's street), it is actually named after a medieval alderman called Kynge.

When the French invaders arrived in Carmarthen, they established their new castle on the rocky hilltop overlooking the River Towy. The Romans had established their own riverside port below the hill and the newcomers did the same. At first built in wood but gradually improved and reconstructed with stone, it became one of the most important fortifications in south west Wales. The seat of both political and military power. It was also strongly associated with the administration of justice.

The earliest trials would have taken place here, and the castle also acted as a prison. Television and the cinema have accustomed us to inmates being locked up in unsanitary dungeons and thrown into pestilential cells, and there is no doubt Carmarthen Castle had such accommodation available. However, records tell us that on occasion there were as many as eighty or more prisoners to be kept alongside the building's regular inhabitants. Accounts from 1390 suggest that five of the towers held prisoners, with money spent on locks, bolts, fetters, chains and handcuffs. While wealthy prisoners who were held for ransom could expect a reasonable accommodation in accordance with their status, the more lowly had to put up with often appalling conditions. Executions took place in the castle too – the ledgers for 1491 mention the cost of building new gallows. There is also sundry spending on stocks for holding minor offenders.

Outside the castle gates, the market square seems to have been a place of punishment in medieval and

Tudor times, with contemporary maps appearing to show both stocks and the pillory. They also indicate the site of the Market Cross, a place now occupied by the statue of Sir William Nott. A much smaller memorial underneath the statue records the death there in March 1555 of Dr Robert Ferrar, who was the Bishop of St David's. He was one of more than three hundred Protestant martyrs who were killed during the reign of Queen Mary for their support of Protestant reforms to the church.

A series of show trials ended with a hearing in the Consistory Court in St Peter's Church, where Dr Ferrar was sentenced to death. Before his execution the bishop declared that his belief in his own faith was so strong that he would go to his death without showing any of the signs of the agonies he was about to endure. He told a spectator, "if he saw him once stir in the pains of his burning, he might then give no credit to his doctrine."

The Bishop was chained to a post and bundles of wood were placed around his feet; the time came for the bonfire to be lit. At this point the High Sheriff, who was supervising the execution, discovered a snag. He had forgotten to arrange for someone to carry out the lighting of the fire.

When none of his own soldiers could be persuaded to do it, he called for a volunteer from the crowd who were watching in silence. Although the Yorkshire-born bishop was not a particularly popular man in south Wales, the onlookers were sympathetic to the poor man's plight.

Again, when no one came forward to volunteer, the sheriff was forced to offer a bribe. He promised to reward the executioner with the gift of a small farm. It proved an irresistible offer to a poor farmworker who agreed to light the bonfire.

However, once the fire was lit and the flames began to burn the bishop's clothes and singe his hair and beard, the poor peasant ran from the square "weeping copiously." The would-be farmer never got to enjoy his reward. Foxe's *Book of Martyrs* reports that he died a day or so later of what was called "apoplexy" – these days more commonly diagnosed as a stroke or heart attack.

In the meantime, it was obvious to all the onlookers that the bishop must have been suffering terribly in the flames. Yet, true to his word, he made not a sound nor gave any indication of the severity of his burns.

Among the crowd was a soldier called Richard Gravell who took pity on the Bishop. Borrowing a pikestaff from one of the troops guarding the bonfire, the officer got close enough to the flames to strike the poor man over the head, putting an end to his suffering.

The execution is marked by a small plaque that records: "Near this spot suffered for the truth Dr Robert Ferrar, Bishop of St David's. We shall by God's grace light such a candle in England as will never be put out."

While the gallows and the stake claimed serious offenders, the square was also the place for the punishment of minor misdemeanors. The victim would be forced to stand at the pillory with wrists and head held in place by a hinged wooden board. Public humiliation formed part of the penance, although the severity of that punishment depended on the mood of the onlookers. Crowds would often laugh and jeer at the prisoner as well as pelting them with dung, offal, rotten vegetables and, on occasions, sticks and stones.

The uncompromising Unitarian preacher Tomos Glyn Cothi is supposedly the last to suffer in this way in 1813. The authorities regarded him as a dangerous supporter of French republicanism who had dared to preach revolution in this country. In 1802 he was committed to Carmarthen Gaol for singing an adaptation of the new French anthem *La Marseillaise* calling for the liberty of the poor. He used his time in prison to write a Welsh-English dictionary.

On the day he went to the pillory, he bought himself a new waistcoat and jacket and, once locked in, his daughter stood by his side. A woman in the crowd threw a rotten egg at his head, to the great displeasure of the other onlookers, who turned on her. Cothi then spent the rest of his time in the pillory preaching his usual brand of sedition, to the fury of the authorities.

By the time of Cothi's imprisonment, Carmarthen Castle had all but disappeared. All that remained of the once mighty fortress were ruined walls and towers. In its place stood a brand-new prison, designed by one of Britain's foremost architects.

The castle's destruction came as a result of the Civil Wars that tore the country apart during the seventeenth century. At the start of the conflict, the castle was in the hands of forces loyal to King Charles I, and Wales was predominantly a royalist nation. However, the Parliamentary forces controlled the Navy, and in 1644 they landed an army by ship to seize the castle.

The Roundheads held it during the winter months, but in the spring the king's men returned and recaptured it, enclosing the town in an earthen rampart to protect it from future attack. The remains of the earthworks can still be seen from the footpath linking Lammas Street to the town park and velodrome. Despite the improved fortifications, the Royalist garrison gave up the castle again and surrendered after a siege by the parliamentarians lasting only one week.

The war came to an end and King Charles fled to France to escape retribution. Parliament discharged the army without paying the troops for their service. Colonel John Poyer, who led the Roundhead forces in south Wales, organised a petition calling for the men to be paid, but the government refused. Poyer and his followers then declared themselves for the King, Charles returned from exile in France and the second stage of the Civil War began.

Oliver Cromwell was the soldier charged with defeating the rebels. A skilled general, he fought them from town to town, defeating his opponents and

The Castle Gateway.

destroying the fortifications used by his enemies to prevent them being used again.

Carmarthen Castle was abandoned without being attacked but, to prevent it falling again into rebel hands, Cromwell ordered the buildings to be "slighted," the name given to the process of blowing up the walls and defensive towers with gunpowder. Cromwell is reported to have stood at the end of St Mary's Street watching the destruction.

After the conflict, with Charles beheaded at Whitehall, the army dealt with the former rebels. The ordinary soldiers were allowed to go free, with all the blame firmly attached to the three rebel leaders. Colonels John Poyer, Rice Powell and Major General Roland Laugharne were found guilty of treason and sentenced to death.

However, General Fairfax, who commanded the Roundhead forces, declared that he still had use for the officers who had proved themselves worthy opponents in battle provided they agreed to serve in the new Commonwealth army. Nevertheless, he declared that one general had to die, and ordered them to decide who it would be. The officers refused to make that decision, so Fairfax made them draw lots to decide who was to live and who to die. Poyer lost and was executed by firing squad in front of a huge crowd in London's Covent Garden.

The remains of Carmarthen Castle then became the county gaol, with the inmates held captive among the ruins. Only the Gatehouse was in a fit state to be used for the purpose and conditions were generally pretty miserable, with no water supply, cold and damp cells and earthen floors. Men, women and children were forced to share the same wretched accommodation. When the prisoner reformer John Howard visited, he found the place to be cramped and "offensive." However, there were only between eleven and twenty-two prisoners normally held here. The town of Carmarthen had its own gaol at Prisoners' Gate which stood between the Market Place and King Street.

The inmates were kept in cells over the gateway with a flight of thirteen stone steps leading from the street level up to the prison doorway. Debtors as well as ordinary criminals were kept here, and they would often beg for food, lowering baskets down from the cell windows and begging passersby to put money or bread into them. Local children were warned to behave themselves – "otherwise you will find yourself going up the thirteen steps." Although the gateway and prison were demolished around 250 years ago, the expression was still in use as recently as this decade.

Following Howard's report on both gaols, a new prison was commissioned. To build it the council turned to an architect called John Nash, who these days is more famous for the many stately homes he built around Britain, including Buckingham Palace and the Prince Regent's Pavilion in Brighton.

The high costs of divorce had driven Nash from London to Carmarthen. He had worked here as an apprentice when the new Guildhall was built, so knew the area well and he had been left a small piece of woodland at Taliaris by a relative.

His wife Jane had not only run up a fortune in dressmaker's bills in the capital, but had also fooled Nash into believing he was the father of two babies she had adopted. During the supposed pregnancy, she had put padding under her clothes to simulate pregnancy and had paid to buy the children from their willing mothers. Discovering the fraud, Nash packed his wife off to stay with relatives at Aberavon, where she embarked on a scandalous affair with one of her husband's friends, a dancing teacher called Charles Charles. When local cockle pickers discovered the couple making love on the beach, Nash demanded a divorce. Charles Charles was sued for damages and, unable to pay, died in a debtor's prison.

Once settled in Carmarthen, Nash first worked on improvements to St Peter's Church before turning his hand to prison building. The prison proved to be a considerable improvement on the former establishment. It boasted separate cells for men, women and children as well as for debtors, an infirmary was provided for the sick, and exercise yards and a garden offered the inmates time in the fresh air. One wall of Nash's prison still survives, between the County Hall car park and the former Victorian police station, with evidence of the infirmary windows still visible in the stonework.

Hard labour was the order of the day for the felons, who were given comparatively short sentences but were expected to work at some task suited to their age and aptitude during their confinement. Tasks ranged from stepping on the treadmill to breaking stones for road making. Some of the cells had a crank handle attached to a box fitted against the wall. Inmates had to turn the handle hundreds of times during the day to earn food to enhance the basic prison diet. Prison warders supervised the task and were able to make the task easier or more difficult by turning a screw on the side of the box – earning officers the nickname "screws."

One governor of the prison made the prisoners work to create a private garden in an unusual location. They were made to fill up the walls of the largest remaining tower with stone and then earth almost to the top. The small garden they created can still be accessed by a steep stone staircase beyond a metal gate in the corner of the council car park.

Prison reforms in the 1850s put an end to John Nash's prison, although the distinctive gatehouse survived, being used to house women prisoners. A new set of buildings replaced it: a grim Victorian block consisting of three separate wings for the male inmates with a new treadmill and outbuildings housing the kitchen and laundry. It was topped by a huge chimneystack which dominated the Carmarthen skyline until the building was demolished in the 1930s.

When County Hall, which now occupies the site, was built in the 1940s and 50s, there were plans to save Nash's Georgian gatehouse. The stones were carefully dismantled and numbered to facilitate their rebuilding, only for their location to be lost during the turmoil of the Second World War.

Oddly enough, County Hall still retains a set of dungeons. Originally it was thought the Council Chamber could serve a dual purpose as a courthouse. In the basement is a set of cells, never used to hold prisoners, now employed as a secure space to store council archives.

THE
WILD WEST

Carmarthen today is a peaceful town, by and large. Things may get a little lively on Friday and Saturday nights around some of the busier pubs and clubs, but for the most part it's a law-abiding and friendly place. So it is perhaps a little hard to believe that we once had the justifiable reputation of being the wildest town in Wales.

Two street names hold a clue to our violent past. Red and Blue Streets, meeting together either side of Dark Gate at the lower end of Guildhall Square, are both colourful reminders of a period in Carmarthen's political history when riots, intimidation, corruption and mob violence were a regular part of urban life.

The trouble began with intense political rivalry between the county's most powerful landowners. The Red faction claimed allegiance to the Tories, while the Blue faction was aligned with the Whigs. In Carmarthen only a few hundred of the very wealthiest landowners and traders had the right to vote, but each side was backed by sections of the local population who formed themselves into huge mobs to support their favoured candidates.

From the early years of the eighteenth century, elections in the town were marked by violence on a massive scale. One held in 1796 saw a man shot, windows and bones broken, and houses of known supporters of one side or the other demolished by rioters or set on fire. The troublemakers were generally drawn from the poorer sections of the town: sailors, fishermen, coracle men and their families who, with little else to entertain them, took to violence with enthusiasm.

Bribery and corruption were rife at election times, with the most notorious example being Y Lecsiwn Fawr – the Great Election – of 1802. The Whig candidate was Sir William Paxton, said to be the wealthiest man in the country. He had recently built a magnificent mansion at Middleton Hall, now the site of the National Botanic Garden of Wales, and aimed to become the town's MP.

As part of his campaign he paid for 11,070 breakfasts, 36,901 dinners, 684 suppers, 25,275 gallons of beers, 11,068 bottles of whisky, 8,879 bottles of strong ale, 460 bottles of sherry and 509 bottles of cider. With fewer than five hundred eligible to vote, most of the food and booze went to placate the so-called "Carmarthen Mob." It cost Paxton almost sixteen thousand pounds, a massive sum at a time when a labourer's wage would be around twenty pounds a year. He also pledged to build a new and much-needed bridge across the Towy if he was elected. Having spent a fortune, Sir William lost the election by sixty votes! Legend has it that, in a fit of pique, he spent the money he promised for the new bridge on building a monument in memory of Admiral Lord Nelson, a tower now known as Paxton's Folly, which stands overlooking the Towy Valley. Having been taught a valuable lesson about the perils of trying to bribe the electorate, he was ultimately forgiven by the town and elected Mayor of Carmarthen the following year.

Social unrest across Europe, typified by the revolution in France, was causing great changes in society and the emerging middle class agitated for political reform and the right to vote. At the same time, soaring food prices in the period after the Napoleonic Wars caused great hardship, leading to what became known as the Carmarthen Cheese Riots of 1818.

Volcanic eruptions in the Dutch East Indies forced tons of dust particles into the stratosphere, effectively blocking out the sun and creating in 1817 "the year without a summer." Cool temperatures and heavy rain resulted in failed harvests across Europe and the price of bread and other staple food soared. In 1818 a group of Carmarthen merchants decided they could get better prices for the locally produced cheeses in cities like London and Bristol and started buying up supplies and putting them into storage, inflating prices and denying local people a favourite food. On the day the cargo of cheese was due to be shipped, a huge but peaceful demonstration, led by a brass band, descended on the harbour. The cheese was removed from the ship's hold, but not stolen – instead the mob returned the cheese to the warehouse and called for it to be sold locally for a fair price.

The merchants then attempted to smuggle the cheese on board ship under cover of darkness, but the protesters had kept watch and a second demonstration stormed the ship to put the cheese back in the warehouse. Eventually the local militia – a part-time military force – succeeded in protecting the cheese and the export went ahead, but this kind of enterprise was never attempted again on such a scale.

Elections in Carmarthen were now even more fiercely contested; none more so than the parliamentary election of 1831 when Carmarthen became the only town in Britain unable to return an MP because of the level of violence. The candidates were John Jones, a local lawyer, for the Reds and a naval captain, John Philipps, for the Blues.

Voting took place in the Guildhall and was carried out in public. Electors stood in the jury box to declare who they were supporting and their vote was recorded by the Town Clerk, with other local officials and representatives of candidates in the courtroom present to see fair play. No sooner had the proceedings opened than a mob of Red supporters stormed the courthouse "conducting themselves in a tumultuous and riotous manner, menacing and threatening all who might come forward as voters for John Johns with the infliction of immediate vengeance."

Amid scenes of chaos, the election was postponed until the next day, only for the situation to deteriorate further. Seventy local men, armed with clubs, had been sworn in as temporary policemen to guard the Guildhall, but the mob swept them away. A local vicar tried to vote and was threatened with death. Then Samuel Rees, a man with just one eye, climbed into the jury box only to be told by one ruffian that if he voted for his chosen candidate, then his other eye would be put out. The unrest continued and the election was abandoned.

Eventually soldiers from Brecon arrived to enforce a kind of peace on the town, but lesser riots and general discontent continued for months. Carmarthen even hired six members of the newly formed Metropolitan Police to help: men who made such a positive impression that the town formed its own police force a few years later. The elections of 1832 were just as violent, with the army and the local militia once again called in to enforce order. However, the passing of the 1832 Reform Act marked a lessening of political tension, and although local rivalries remained, the anger of the mob switched to a new cause of discontent – turnpike tolls.

Parliamentary legislation promoted the building of vital new roads across Britain, but allowed local road-building companies to collect tolls from road users to pay for construction and maintenance.

The insignia for the Carmarthen Constabulary
charged with keeping the peace.

Tollgates were thrown up along the main roads, imposing charges on all the traffic that passed through, from farm carts and horsemen to herds of sheep and cattle. However, greedy investors saw the tolls as a way to make money and began imposing restrictive charges on road users. Farmers suffered more than most and it was said that the cost of a cart load of lime collected from the dock side to improve the fields could increase ten-fold by the time it reached the farm because of the toll charges.

In 1843 tensions came to a head when huge gangs of men began attacking the tollgates at night. Armed with an assortment of tools and weapons and with blackened faces, each mob was led by a "Rebecca": a man dressed as a woman, often sporting a longhaired wig.

Typical of their attacks was one carried out on the Water Street Gate in Carmarthen. On 27th May Henry Thomas, the gate keeper, woke to find a mob of three hundred of Rebecca's "sisters" on his doorstep. He begged them not to destroy his furniture or harm his family. Because he had offered no resistance to them, they left his own property alone, but began removing the roof of the tollhouse and destroying the tollgate. The noise attracted the attention of the newly-formed police force. All five of them rushed to the scene of the crime and were met by continual shotgun fire from "sisters" concealed along Water Street. Their task completed, Rebecca and her supporters retreated to the countryside around Talog and Newchurch, firing gunshots as they went.

Not all of Rebecca's supporters were willing accomplices. The more law-abiding citizens were threatened with violence if they paid the toll gate fees. One sign distributed in the countryside warned: "the goods of all persons who will henceforth pay at the Water Street Gate will be burned and their lives taken from them, Beca." Faced with these threats, three local men refused to pay at the temporary gate created as a replacement. Fined heavily by the town magistrates, the men were ordered by the Rebeccaites not to pay. As a result, police and bailiffs were sent to seize property equal to the value of the fines. But on their way back to Carmarthen they found themselves surrounded by Rebecca and four hundred of her "children," many of them armed with guns. The hapless policemen were made to give up the goods they had seized and then forced to walk to the country home of the chief magistrate where they were ordered to demolish the walls of his estate.

With attacks on tollgates around the county continuing, news reached the authorities of plans to hold a huge demonstration in Carmarthen on Monday 19th June. Faced with massive public unrest, the mayor sent for the army and a troop of the 4th Light Dragoons was sent from Cardiff to deal with the protestors.

The Rebeccaites assembled at the Plough and Harrow inn on the Cynwyl Elfed road at eleven in the morning. Around three hundred horsemen and another two-and-a-half-thousand supporters on foot set off for the town centre. With no sign yet of the army, a courageous group of magistrates tried to get the crowd to turn back, but were ignored. As the demonstration approached Carmarthen, they were joined by hundreds of townspeople who completely filled Guildhall Square, leaving little room for the protestors to pass through.

Having made their point, the mob then turned their attention to another object of hate for the poorer sections of society – the Union Workhouse on Penlan Hill. Only the most desperate among the poor would apply to join the other paupers who were housed there. The regime was severe; married couples were forced to live apart in prison-like conditions. Their children were also held in separate quarters. Food and clothing were provided, but the inmates had to work hard for their keep, forced to break stones for road-building.

Some local opinion had it that "idle vagabonds" would commit petty offences with the sole purpose of being sent to prison, where the food and accommodation were far superior to what they normally had. One Carmarthen magistrate suggested that rather than send such individuals to prison, they should be given "a sound, hearty thrashing which will, no doubt, have the desired effect" of dissuading people from offending again.

Now the demonstrators stormed the workhouse, terrorising not only the staff, but the inmates as well.

Horrible the conditions might have been, but for the poor who lived there, this was their home. While the male paupers managed to keep the rioters at bay, other protestors ran amock in the children's and women's quarters, throwing furniture, bedding and blankets out of the windows and preparing to burn the place down.

It was at this point that the Dragoons arrived on the scene. Blistering hot weather had delayed the troops on their journey from their temporary lodgings in Llandeilo. They had ridden their horses so hard in the heat that several of them had collapsed of exhaustion and died. Now they galloped across the town bridge, up Castle Hill and onto Spilman Street where the magistrates, gathered at the Ivy Bush, told them the workhouse was under attack. Led by magistrate Thomas Morris, shouting "slash away, slash away," the soldiers drew their sabres and charged up Penlan Hill. The result was instant panic as the crowd began to flee, scrambling through hedges, fields and gardens to try and escape. Miraculously no one was badly hurt as the authorities succeeded in restoring order, arresting some sixty men who were immediately questioned by the magistrates in a temporary court held in the workhouse schoolroom. Every man told the same story: they had been forced to take part in the demonstration by threats of having their homes burnt down and their lives taken.

However, the military action put an end to the activities of Rebecca in Carmarthen, although there were continuing incidents throughout the county over the following months. More soldiers and fifty London policemen were drafted in to restore order to the countryside and to impose the rule of law.

By the time the rioters came to trial the following spring, the government and the courts had recognised that the protestors had genuine grievances. The Turnpike Acts of 1844 lowered the tolls and discontent faded. Those local men who faced the courts were handed lenient sentences of just eight months hard labour; unpleasant, but more merciful than the order for transportation to Australia awarded elsewhere in the country.

DEVIL'S DAY

If Carmarthen folk were capable of riotous behaviour in support of political causes, they threw just as much energy into enjoying themselves. Every opportunity was taken to celebrate events of every kind, from a good hanging to the coronation of a new king.

Bad news was marked by communal inebriation; good news toasted by one and all.

The death of Admiral Lord Nelson at the Battle of Trafalgar in 1805 combined both tragedy and victory, leaving the authorities with a dilemma. Should they ring out the church bells to celebrate the navy's success or toll the mourning bell to mark Nelson's passing? The national hero had visited Carmarthen in 1802, stayed in town and lodged at the Ivy Bush in the company of his lover, Lady Emma Hamilton and her elderly husband, Sir William. The admiral and his lady made for a contrasting couple; he was tall and stick thin while the once-celebrated beauty was now short and enormously fat. A civic dinner was thrown in Nelson's honour and the visitors joined the audience in the New Theatre, attracting crowds wherever they went. When news reached Carmarthen of both the victory and Nelson's death, a compromise was reached: the bells were rung in celebration for fifteen minutes, then tolled for a further quarter-of-an-hour. The whole process then was repeated every half-hour throughout the day.

At the time, you could have toasted the admiral's victory in any one of Carmarthen's one hundred and fifty pubs, gin-shops or alehouses – roughly one for every forty inhabitants. The number of customers would have swelled on market days when thousands packed into the pubs, not to mention thirsty sailors spending time in the busy port while their cargoes were unloaded.

Alcohol was at the centre of town life and Carmarthen had a well-deserved reputation for drunkenness. One national weekly newspaper declared that the town "possessed the most drunken inhabitants in Wales."

When the temperance movement gained support throughout the country in the latter part of the nineteenth century, the Salvation Army held Carmarthen as an example of a place where alcohol abuse was rife. One of their number reported that during visits on two Sundays, he saw more drunkenness in town than he had seen in the whole of Swansea in six months. It did not escape notice that this was at a time when the pubs in Wales were supposed to be "dry" – that is, closed on Sundays.

The Carmarthen Weekly Reporter commented: "It is called the Lord's Day, but in Carmarthen it is par excellence the Devil's Day. Not only the law of the land but the Ten Commandments are regarded as suspended for the time being by a very large proportion of the population."

Although the upper classes could be just as boisterous as the poor, with balls and dances held in the coaching inns or at the Assembly Rooms on King Street until the early hours of the morning, it was inevitable that the lower classes were the ones who ended up before the courts as a result of their drunken behaviour. Champion among them was Anne Awberry, a prostitute, who made one hundred and thirty appearances in front of the magistrates charged with being "drunk and riotous." On her final appearance before the bench, PC David James reported: "I saw the defendant on Lammas Street near the Boar's Head Hotel. She was very drunk and singing and making a great noise and creating a disturbance. She has been very bad since she came out of gaol last." Having already spent a major part of her life behind bars, she was committed to Carmarthen Prison yet again, this time for three months.

Men could also be prolific offenders; James Davies, a wool carder, chalked up seventy-three convictions for drunkenness, while Daniel Jones, a shoemaker of Catherine Street, managed ninety-seven appearances before the magistrates.

One night of the year when everyone joined in

The Boar's Head Hotel
on Lammas Street.

with the revels was Christmas Eve, celebrated in Carmarthen as "Torch Night." The evening was marked with wild and drunken behaviour, given an extra edge of danger by the activities that surrounded it. Gangs roamed the streets carrying blazing torches, firing guns into the air. Fireworks were thrown and flaming tar-barrels rolled through the streets. One favourite sport was kicking off two empty beer barrels from Nott Square, one sent downhill along St Mary's Street, the other one down Guildhall Street, to see which arrived in Guildhall Square first – and woe betide anyone who got in the way! Torch Night survived until 1870, when the mayor called for the tradition to end because of the chaos the event caused.

Who could blame the poor for seeking some relief from their suffering in the glass and in boisterous behaviour? In the early years of the nineteenth century, one third of the town's population existed at a subsistence level with four to five families crammed together in tiny cottages, sleeping seven or eight people to a bed. One in three children died before they reached the age of five and the average life expectancy was just forty-one years. One local undertaker, working in the middle years of the nineteenth century, reported that almost forty-per-cent of his work was burying children under the age of ten. Half of his "clients" died before reaching their twentieth birthday.

The poverty was most acute among the coracle men and their families who mainly lived in the Dan y

Banc area of the town. They scraped as good a living as they could catching sewin (sea trout) or salmon in the Towy.

Speaking their own language, a form of medieval Welsh, they had strictly enforced codes for fishing the river that determined exactly when and where they could cast their nets. There was a fierce rivalry between the coracle men who fished the river and the fishermen in the Towy estuary between Ferryside and Llansteffan who used Seine-nets to harvest fish. They often argued very publicly over where the boundary line should be between the two activities. One clash developed in 1864 when fishermen working on the Towy between Pilroath and Pilglas noticed a small flotilla of coracles heading towards them. The coracle men began a fight, ripping the hated Seine-net to pieces during the process. The attackers landed seven days hard-labour as a reward, which normally meant serving that time on the treadmill. This would have posed a problem for one of them, one-legged Billy Owen, who doubtless was given an alternative punishment.

A few years earlier a similar confrontation had developed into a full-scale fight dubbed the "Battle of Banc yr Alma" after a major battle recently reported to have taken place during the Crimean War. This time both men and women clashed on a sandbank revealed by the low tide. The combatants wielded a wide assortment of weapons, including the small clubs used to stun the fish. Bones had already been broken and blood spilt before a gunshot rang out. One of the Ferryside women had been hit by shotgun pellets and fell to the ground. Realising things had gone too far, the combatants scattered. Legend has it that the coracle man who had fired the shot fled the scene and then the country, making for America where he married and raised a family.

One way of augmenting the coracle men's income was by hauling in a bigger catch; the coroner paid a bounty to those who collected corpses from the river. Bathing accidents, suicides, falls from the quay and ships would all contribute to the harvest of bodies. Where the corpse was landed decided the coroner's fee. Those landed in the Borough of Carmarthen were rewarded with seven shillings and six pence, while those taken ashore in the county got twelve and six. Naturally, most bodies were towed to the county bank.

Among them was Kate Bear, a prostitute nicknamed "Beelzebub," who drowned in July 1891. She had picked up a sailor from a German ship, the "Alpha." Making her way onboard, she overbalanced and fell in the river, drowning in the strong current. Her body was found the following morning on a sandbank by two coracle fishermen who arranged for her body to be landed by boat at Pothouse Wharf.

Given the perilous way the men were forced to scrape a living, it is small wonder that many of them some sought relief from their poverty by signing up to the army. In 1846 a recruiting party scoured the pubs and alehouses for new soldiers. The team, made up of an officer, sergeant, drummer and flag-bearer, were flush with cash and prepared to buy drinks for likely candidates in the hope that they would sign up to the regimental colours.

They found a young man called Benny Hat Wen drinking with his mates and soon got him drunk enough to accept the Queen's Shilling. Taking the coin from the officer or sergeant was believed to be a legal contract. With the coin is his hand, Benny soon sobered up. There was no way he wanted to leave his family and friends in Carmarthen and go abroad to die. How the heck could he get out of this?

Benny reckoned that the army would not want a handicapped man. So he took out the pocket knife that all young men carried in those days and tried to cut off his trigger finger. His friends were horrified and took the knife from him. He then tried unsuccessfully to bite off the end of his finger. When that failed, he made his way to the back yard where the landlord kept an axe for chopping firewood and used that to do the deed.

No finger. But no army service either. Benny was right, the army did not want to enlist a handicapped man into their ranks. He celebrated his escape from military service by getting thoroughly drunk. Other Carmarthen men were happy to serve in the forces, although some never had the chance to see their hometown again.

The navy also looked to Carmarthen to fill up the gaps in its ranks. The Press Gangs were allowed by law to seize "eligible men of seafaring habits between the ages of eighteen and fifty-five years," and the town, as one of the busiest ports in south Wales, would have made an attractive target. In 1803 they raided Carmarthen, but were spotted as they approached. The town bells were rung out as a warning to sailors to hide, although non-seafarers were also occasionally kidnapped. The navy was empowered to use force during "impressment," but on this occasion, they were thwarted by the women of the town who formed a mob to attack the sailors and drive them away empty handed.

The violence and savagery that often marked public celebrations of every kind in Carmarthen was often mirrored in the cruelty of the entertainments on offer in the town. While the wealthy could enjoy shooting parties and riding to hounds, the poorer population had their own blood sports to amuse them. None was more popular than the centuries' old practice of bull-baiting.

The bull was tethered to a stake to prevent it from moving away from the scene of the fight. Trained bulldogs were unleashed and set upon the poor creature, with the watching crowds betting on the outcome of the contest.

Points were scored as the dogs attempted to bite the bull and hang on to the flesh. Carmarthen was famous for the quality of those bulldogs that were trained to sink their teeth into the bull's nose, attracting the highest score. The bull meanwhile, primed for the fight by having pepper blown into its nostrils, would do its best to shake off the attackers, often killing or maiming them in the process, using both hooves and horns to try to inflict damage on his tormentors.

In Carmarthen, bull baiting usually took place outside the Guildhall where the town council had paid for chains and a metal spike to be set into the cobbles. Butchers would happily provide the bulls for the competition in the belief that the baiting helped to tenderise the meat before slaughter. Hugely popular events, they would attract large crowds to the square.

In 1805 those crowds proved the undoing of the landlord of the Boar's Head Hotel. In the great press of people anxious to see the fight, the man was pushed too close to the bull. It tossed its great head and, in the process, one of the bull's horns slashed into the innkeeper's stomach. Weeping from his wounds and suffering in agony, he was carried back to his hotel where it took him three days to die. His ghost is still believed to haunt the premises today. Some claim his ghastly moans can still be heard echoing through the hotel.

POLICEMEN, PUBS
&
PROSTITUTES

"**P**rostitution is on the increase in the town of Carmarthen," Canon Camber Williams told an enthralled audience in Swansea in 1906. They were assembled to raise funds to help rescue these "fallen women."

"There has been an immense and terrible increase in the sin of impurity," he reported. "Hundreds of little girls are going down the road of sin and ruin in our town." It was ever thus. Throughout the nineteenth century, and doubtless long before, Carmarthen was a town famous for its prostitutes and brothels. As a centre for military life, a busy port and thriving market town, there was always a demand for the so-called "nymphs of the pavement" or "frail sisterhood," as the women were known.

Desperate conditions for the poor would have helped to swell their numbers, but there is equally no doubt that market forces were at work, and there was a keen demand for prostitution among the men who flocked to the town for both business and pleasure.

If Carmarthen men were notorious for drunkenness and riotous behaviour, there is little doubt that their womenfolk were just as enthusiastic.

Back gardens, sheltered doorways, parks and gardens were all utilised in the throes of passion. Even the town's graveyards were not immune. In 1884 Thomas Thomas faced the magistrates at the Guildhall and was fined for having intercourse "with a woman of low character" among the gravestones at St Peter's church. However, there were also plenty of brothels to be found among the Carmarthen cottages and common lodging houses, and the town's many public houses often served a dual purpose. When the police raided the Bird In Hand after a complaint from the mother of one of the working girls employed there, they found a couple in one bedroom and two men and one woman in another.

"There were a tremendous number of fellows who went upstairs at a fee of one shilling a time," Carmarthen Police Court was told by a witness. They fined the landlord William Evans twenty pounds and sentenced him to two months' hard labour.

The services of the prostitutes were never more in demand than when the militia were on training manoeuvres in the area, attracting women from as far afield as Ireland and Cardiff to work in Carmarthen for the duration. The magistrates did their best to stem the tide of prostitution; Anne Awberry, an enthusiastic and ageing prostitute and notorious town drunk, was set free one New Year in the forlorn hope that she would now turn over a new leaf, while another girl, labelled "young in years though old in iniquity," was discharged from the court with the words "go and sin no more" ringing in her ears.

Carmarthen's small police force was also continually troubled by the antics of the call girls, although it was only when they were involved in acts of theft or drunken violence that they normally fell afoul of the law. On occasion, the police were found to have had a closer association with the prostitutes than their superiors would have liked.

The town got its first taste of modern policing during the political riots of 1831 when the town employed members of the newly formed Metropolitan Police to help bring calm to the streets. The handful of disciplined and uniformed officers made a strong impression on local politicians, who resolved to establish a force of their own. Before then, policing was an ad hoc affair that relied on concerned citizens to bring most villains to justice.

Night watchmen, given the collective nickname "Wil y Lon," patrolled the streets at night. These elderly men, who were usually retired soldiers, were tasked with reporting any criminal acts to the mayor the next day. Special constables or a part-time "watch" were drafted in to apprehend more serious offenders, with the army or local militia called upon in the case of public disorder.

Carmarthen's new town police force was established in 1835, comprising of a chief constable, three full-time constables and eight others who worked only part-time. The force remained at that size, bar a few years during the Second World War, right up until it was merged with the county police in 1947. At some stage they earned the nickname "The Carmarthen Shilling" because there were twelve coppers on the force. Police had earned the nickname of "copper" because they "copped" – that is, arrested criminals, while twelve copper pennies made up one old fashioned shilling.

The first policemen were hardly the upstanding individuals we might expect today. Instead they were drawn from the Carmarthen Mob who had rioted so enthusiastically a few years before. The town council wanted "bruisers" who had the strength and power to battle against the often drunken offenders they would encounter on the streets and in the pubs; who better than those who could hold their own in a fight?

It was alcohol that often proved their undoing in the early years of the force. Within the first five years of its existence, twelve members of the core police force lost their jobs due to drunkenness. The Watch Committee decided in 1840 that "in future any police constable reported as having been in a public house or off his beat, being sober he be fined two shillings … if drunk, to be dismissed."

Although the threat of dismissal was undoubtedly a deterrent, many of the constables were still sorely tempted. One of the first sergeants, David Williams, reported that he found PC Thomas under the influence of liquor during the early part of his shift.

Later he discovered him in a brothel, too drunk to stand. He took the constable home where, as they tried to undress him, he attacked both his sergeant and his wife. Despite all of this, PC Thomas still managed to hold on to his job.

No doubt the alcohol was a welcome relief, given the hard conditions of their working life. The hours were long and the pay miserable, and the threat of drunken violence being inflicted on them was a constant danger. Typical was an encounter between Sergeant John Davies and a coracle man named John Lewis, whom the policeman found "very drunk, cursing and swearing and disorderly."

The Police Constabulary at Castle House Lock-up.

Mr Lewis was taken into custody after he refused to go home peacefully, according to the Sergeant's report. The man resisted arrest and violently assaulted the officer, kicking his legs and causing a mass of cuts and bruises. Lewis then punched the sergeant, spat in his face and bit his hand. The coracle man next tried to strangle the officer by twisting the collar of his uniform. Fortunately for the sergeant, the attempt to throttle him failed when the hooks that held the collar in place gave way. Lewis was finally subdued when the police were forced to use their truncheons.

Sometimes the police were a little rough and ready, often happy to send a drunk on their way with a clip around the ear rather than go to the trouble of taking them into custody. Occasionally they used their powers to extort a little money on the side. One constable, David Rees, was suspended from duty after it became known that he had helped out "a common woman of the town" known as "Betsy Cow." Betsy had fallen pregnant and asked PC Rees to get some compensation from the unwitting father-to-be. The constable managed to extract one pound from the man, giving fifteen shillings to Betsy but keeping five shillings for himself.

The relationship between the police and the prostitutes was sometimes even closer. The *Carmarthen Journal* reported that one businessman who was fresh off the coach from Gloucester got thoroughly drunk and was found wandering the streets at three o'clock in the morning, much the worse for wear and demanding to know where he could "meet with some women of loose character." The helpful constable led the traveller to a brothel on Lammas Street where, later in the night, one of the girls stole gold sovereigns from the pockets of his trousers that had been left hanging over a chair.

In 1851 the public was scandalised when PC Thomas Phillips married one of the "nymphs," only to discover that she was already married. Later evidence given in court revealed that the policeman was, in fact, the fourth man to marry her after falling for her charms. It caused so much interest that the public square outside the courtroom in the Guildhall was packed with curious onlookers hoping to catch a glimpse of the woman as she was led away to serve a six-month sentence for bigamy in Carmarthen gaol.

There was further scandal when the police investigation into her case revealed that the woman in question was employed in a brothel owned by another member of the town force; he was given one month to rid himself of this part-time employment, or face dismissal.

According to legend, one Carmarthen girl who fell into a life of prostitution became the final victim of Britain's most notorious murderer, Jack the Ripper.

Although the details are sketchy and difficult to confirm, it is believed that Mary Jane Kelly arrived in the town in the late 1860s. She was said to be one of the seven children of an Irishman from Limerick who found a job working in an iron foundry. Brought up to speak and read Welsh, she is believed to have married a coal miner either in the Carmarthen or Llanelli area when she was about sixteen years of age.

Widowed following an accident at her husband's pit, she is then thought to have taken a job in the Stepney Hotel in Llanelli working as a maid. Tempted by the offer of easy money to eke out her wages, she turned to casual prostitution among the visiting commercial travellers. Those who knew her believe that she then moved to either Swansea or Cardiff before being lured by the bright lights of London.

What little is known about Mary Jane mainly comes from a young man called Joseph Barnett, who lived with the girl until a few weeks before her murder. The information that he passed on comes from Kelly herself and may possibly have been embellished more than a little along the way. It seems likely that she invented some of her personal history to give an aura of glamour to what must have been a hard and unpleasant life. It is also possible that Mr Barnett himself filled in some of the gaps in her life story to earn an extra shilling or two when talking to journalists.

Certainly Mary Jane was a very pretty girl, tall and pleasantly plump, and quite a few years younger and more attractive than the Ripper's other victims. One of her friends described her as "a good, quiet and pleasant girl who was well liked by all of us."

Maria Harvey, another prostitute, said that she was "much superior to that of most persons of her position in life." An acquaintance, Mrs McCarthy, described her as being "an excellent scholar and an artist of no mean degree." Yet, despite her accomplishments, her one-time lover says that she was unable to read English. Clearly a cut above the other local prostitutes, her inability to read seems strange until another of her skills is mentioned: Mary Jane Kelly spoke fluent Welsh. It may well be that, having been brought up in Carmarthen, she learnt to read and write in Welsh rather than English.

Her self-described history had her arriving in London in 1884, aged about 21 years and at the height of her beauty. Calling herself "Marie Jeanette" and "Ginger," she worked in a high-class West End brothel where she met a wealthy gentleman who encouraged her to move to Paris with him. However, the move was short-lived and she returned to London. The next few years saw her living with a variety of men, moving a little lower down the social scale with each new relationship until she was working on the streets and drinking heavily.

By November 1888 she was living in a small bedroom at number 13 Millers Gate in Spitalfields, behind with the rent and so short of money that she was seen begging for the few pence she needed to buy her final meal of fish and chips.

She was last seen alive in the early hours of Friday 9th November in the company of a prosperous-looking gentleman she was kissing and leading towards her home. The following morning her body was discovered when her landlord called to collect the overdue rent. Unable to get a reply when he knocked on the door, the man peered through the window and saw her lying dead on her blood-soaked bed.

As with the other victims of Jack the Ripper, her body had been horribly mutilated, utterly horrifying those officials who had to view the scene of the murder. Her killer has, of course, never been identified, although speculation remains to this day as to his true identity. No family member attended her funeral and her body lies buried in St Patrick's Cemetery in Leytonstone.

Further Reading

Russell Davies, *Secret Sins: Sex, Violence and Society in Carmarthenshire,* University of Wales, Cardiff, 2012

Susan Fern, *The Man Who Killed Richard III,* Amberley, Stroud, 2014

Peter Goodall, *The Black Flag Over Carmarthen,* Gwasg Carreg Gwalch, Llanrwst, 2005

Russell Grigg, *The Little Book of Carmarthen,* History Press, Stroud, 2015

Eric Hughes, *Kidwelly – Memories of Yesteryear,* Dinefwr Press, Llandybie, 2003

Lynn Hughes, *A Carmarthenshire Anthology,* Christopher Davies, Llandybie, 1984

Joyce & Victor Lodwick, *The Story of Carmarthen,* St Peters Press, Carmarthen, 1972

Neil Ludlow, *Carmarthen Castle,* University of Wales Press, Cardiff, 2014

Arthur Mee, *Carmarthenshire Notes Vols 1, 2 & 3,* Carmarthenshire CC, Carmarthen, 1997

Pat Molloy, *A Shilling for Carmarthen,* Gomer Press, Llandysul, 1980

Pat Molloy, *Four Cheers for Carmarthen,* Gomer Press, Llandysul, 1981

Pat Molly, *And They Blessed Rebecca,* Gomer Press, Llandysul ,1983

William Spurrell, *Carmarthen And Its Neighbourhood,* Dyfed County Council, 1995

Richard Suggett, *John Nash, Architect in Wales,* National Library of Wales, Aberystwyth 1995